Postcards to Ma

Martin Stannard

Leafe Press

Published by Leafe Press
Nottingham, England.
www.leafepresspoetry.com

Copyright © Martin Stannard, 2023. All rights reserved.

ISBN: 978-1-7397213-4-3

Postcards to Ma

POSTCARDS TO MA

Sent a picture postcard to Ma "Arrived Safe"
Horse-hauled taxi cart to Hotel Paradiso
("Your Happiness is Our Happiness")
Concierge whispered in one of my two ears
I appear to be 'a man of the world' (I have often
wondered how people see me) If there was
anything he could do or if I felt in need of company
let him know Determined to give him wide berth
for duration of stay The ways of sin are many
while paths of righteousness are bestrewn
with countless corrupt concierges Receptionist
resplendent in crisp white blouse and cosmetics
Room pleasant bathroom well-stocked with toiletries
soap shampoo bath foam oils good quality towels
Egyptian cotton unless I am very much mistaken
Bed comfortable think it's a King though it might be
a Queen I'm not sure but it's pleasingly firm Back
can't stand nights on anything too squishy One reason
I left wife View from window ocean harbour esplanade
promenade concourse cafés bistros Unpacked trunk Noted
good supply of coat hangers in wardrobe alongside
complimentary towelling robe the usual hopeless excuse
for bedroom slippers Pleased chose 4-star not 3-star
You sometimes get what you pay for in this world
Drew up plans itinerary schedule list of things to do
places to go etcetera Light dinner in hotel restaurant
Carrot and ginger velouté followed by coconut and celery
root medallion apple pie and ice cream for pudding
all washed down with Donnhoff Hollenpfad im Muhlenberg
Riesling Compliments to chef via waitress Fifi
To bed with Montaigne's 'Essays' in original Italian
Slept like a library book nobody wants to read
                        Crack of dawn Swam in
ocean Frolicked on sand Sent postcard to Ma
Glad I thought to bring my Olympus OM-D E-M10 Mark IV

although camera creates sorrow or so it's been said
Snapped hospitality staff (i.e. hotel workers in
hotel I'm in Especially receptionist in crisp
white blouse and cosmetics Enjoy tautness
of cotton across generous bosom) but not concierge
also shop keepers market traders street vendors fishermen
stevedores sailors sailors' friends bordello proprietors
working girls (I have often wondered why they look at me
that way) beggars street urchins probably
a couple of drug dealers in there too garbage collectors
secretaries stenographers switchboard
operators clerks Ran out of people turned lens on
architecture What monuments man has raised
unto the heavens Cathedrals churches temples
department stores malls municipal buildings (Town Hall,
police station, jail, lunatic asylum) hospital cinema
public baths strip joints bars dives opium dens mansions
villas condominiums mews cottages apartment blocks
Kept eyes peeled open for balustrades entablatures,
cupolas latticework a colonnade (photography
is thirsty work) porticos spandrels parapets (being
careful not to put head above) crestings and
the most photogenic façades Did not neglect urban
infrastructure which to discerning eye has its own
beauties Highways roads streets boulevards avenues
plazas back-streets alleyways Some dubious
people lurking in some of those There's a railway
so snapped station and sidings and all train-related
appurtenances rolling stock etcetera Not much left
to take Night fell so fell into bed in a dark room
where dreams developed Slept like a folded sheep
                    Crack of dawn Swam in
ocean Frolicked on sand Sent postcard to Ma
Photography has been taken as far as it can
Woke up feeling uncharacteristically philanthropic
Philanthropy never did anyone any harm Visited
local hospital Felt like lending a hand Very run down

(hospital not me I am in the rudest health almost
embarrassingly so) Did what little I could Cured
loads of patients of inter alia Crohn's disease
diphtheria emphysema infectious mononucleosis
arthritis diabetes irritable towel syndrome
depression haemorrhoids low self-esteem
in-growing toenails constipation and its hard-to-spell
opposite chronic obstructive pulmonary disease
lupus shingles psoriasis schizophrenia (had to cure that
one twice) herpes scabies housemaid's knee chlamydia
osteoporosis broken arms legs hearts Could not help but
reflect upon the motives of God inventor of all
suffering Staved off a few cases of definite
imminent death Enjoyed adulation due a medical messiah
(I have often wondered if people see me the same way I see myself)
but didn't enjoy being around so many sick
miserable people Took opportunity to drop in to
research facility of international pharma concern
Very swishy modern shiny postmodern edifice money oozing
out of the walls Assisted in laboratory for an hour or so
Pleased to announce cure for cancer possibly one step nearer and
certainly not further away
Bank account significantly healthier A busy day
Slept like a patient etherised in a 4-star stable
                              Crack of dawn Swam in
ocean Frolicked on sand Sent postcard to Ma
I am questioning the sense I have of sense
(I have often wondered if people see me)
Abandoned plans Made new plans list of things to do
Entered into period of wild experimentation
Began with trying different kinds of lingerie
Thought about wearing make-up but chickened out
Blamed Methodist upbringing Endured a few moments
of despair Didn't enjoy despair so replaced it with
hopelessness Hung around outside public toilets
Noticed how gloomy people entered the lavatories
and how the Sun shone on them as they came out

Made some new friends Collected names telephone numbers
Decided to investigate a range of belief systems and fads
Had a crack (ten minutes each tops) at being agnostic
Buddhist vegan pacifist Marxist epicure internalist
Satanist atheist Christian externalist Irish
Thought about difference between philosophy and religion
and half-baked ideas read about in style magazines
Thought a little bit about possible dietary regimes
Gave up smoking and alcohol Started them again
Life is depressing enough without depriving oneself
of all enjoyment Hit the sack nine hours straight
Absent like a peacock in a bordello Woke to write down
dream diary Woke up to find I dreamed it
                        Crack of dawn Swam in
ocean Frolicked on sand Sent postcard to Ma
Am thinking of you and Democritus the Dog
Sometimes feel brain is underused Sometimes feel brain
has a mind of its own Loitered outside library smoked cigarettes
They say it's bad for you but what's
good for you? Loitered inside library Thought about thinking
Pretty sure thinking ain't what we think
it is Read philosophers thoughtfully
(ten minutes each tops) Made a few notes as follows
Confucius "Life is really simple, but we insist on making it complicated
Plato "I am the wisest man alive, for I know one thing, and
      that is that I know nothing."
Aristotle "There is no great genius without some touch of
      madness."
Kant "What can I know? What ought I to do? What can I hope?"
Socrates "The only true wisdom is in knowing you know nothing."
Nietzsche "You must have chaos within you to give birth
      to a dancing star."
Superman "It doesn't take X-Ray vision to see you are up to
      no good."
Sartre "If you are lonely when you're alone you are in bad
      company."
Hobbes "Curiosity is the lust of the mind."

Mencius "The great man is he who does not lose his child's
    heart."
Epicurus "Nothing is enough for the man to whom enough is
    too little."
Zhuang Zhou "Happiness is the absence of the striving for
    happiness."
Had planned to do 'em in alphabetical order but
recognized futility of following a rigid system
Broke for lunch then
Descartes "Doubt is the origin of wisdom."
Wittgenstein "A serious and good philosophical work
    could be written consisting entirely of jokes."
Hume "Beauty in things exists in the mind which
    contemplates them."
Spinoza "No matter how thin you slice it, there will
    always be two sides."
Locke "The only defence against the world is a thorough
    knowledge of it."
Kierkegaard "Life is not a problem to be solved, but a
    reality to be experienced."
Rousseau "The world of reality has its limits; the world
    of imagination is boundless."
Sun Tzu "In the midst of chaos, there is also
    opportunity."
I'm all over the place going round in circles (I have often
wondered if how people see me is how I really am)
Couldn't decide if the day had been well-spent
or if it had even happened Slept like a monk in a convent
                Crack of dawn Swam in
ocean Frolicked on sand Sent postcard to Ma
After all that brain work changed tack
Signed up for dance lessons ('Special Offer!!!')
Natural grace and elegance will come in useful
also innate sense of rhythm
(I have often wondered if people see the dancer in me)
Soon found there's more to dance than meets the eye
Teacher rattled on about biomechanics musicality

preparation also there was stuff about figures
and movements and patterns To be honest
I can't remember all the words I made
some notes There was the pivot
      the chassé the plier the entendre
      the relever the sauter the tourner
      the glisser the élancer
Can't remember what any of them mean
Should've made better notes Was thinking
I didn't go to dance class to expand my vocabulary
Eventually got around to grabbing a gal and doing some actual danci
Gal by name of Mabel looked better
than a Mabel Eyes reminded me of a lass I knew once
Worked behind the perfume counter at John Lewis
Skin like silk Super superstructure
Danced like an angel on top of a cake
Had a crack (ten minutes each tops) at smooth flow of
foxtrot syncopations of quickstep English Morris
dancing (where all the talk as we pranced was
about the price of beans) the waltz tango and tap
That was just the morning Broke for lunch Afternoon did
the balero mambo rumba It was like being in the
Americas the shuffling feet of the cha cha the hustle
Mabel said she thought the dancing was too sexual
Don't know what she meant
Can't help it if my pants are too tight
Nature will have its say
Then into some fusion bunny hop and watusi
In the evening got down with the youth Learned some
ice cool moves The two-step and Booty pop
      Billy Bounce and scoop arm the hip sway
      the bust down the Biz Markie and the Humpty
Hell of a lively day
Fancied taking Mabel back to the hotel
Husband was waiting for her outside
Back to room alone
Slept like the only pencil in a pencil case

                        Crack of dawn Swam in
ocean Frolicked on sand Sent postcard to Ma
Dancing is mastered Great value for money but I move on
for I am a thoughtful soul Sometimes I think I think
too much Am questioning the question of identity
Who are I? Pondering change of name Hubert Sandie
Colin Alexander Pandora Montague Danielle So many to
choose from April May June Julie Augusta Septimus
Octavia (I have often wondered if people know who I am)
While pondering happened across abundance of
lucrative literary prizes Hefty cheques handed over
to talentless hacks Forgot about changing name
Turned to scribbling for an easy buck Adopted
a *nom de plume* Quickly knocked off first novel
"The Trials of a Genius" Wrote difficult second novel
"More Trials of a Genius" Between novels had a couple
of free days Penned slim volume of award-winning poetry
"The Zenith of Our Feelings" When a man is happy
he writes damn good poetry Was offered post of
Writer-in-Residence at Tourist Information Centre
Declined Accepted instead role of Poet-in-Dormitories
at St. Theresa's Finishing School for Young Ladies
A short-term contract abruptly terminated at lights out
Napped for fifteen hours Slept like a pig in gravy
Dreamed of mermaids in milk
                        Crack of dawn Swam in
ocean Frolicked on sand Sent postcard to Ma
I feel like I don't know enough even though I know
a hell of a lot (I have often wondered if people know me)
Stumbled upon local university whilst out walking
Signed up for Major in History Discovered
time really does fly
Learned about domestication of horse
Invention of the wheel Development of the alphabet
Alexander the Great Greeks Romans etcetera
Aztecs Incas Ghengis Khan Chinese
alchemists seeking elixir of life Inventing

gunpowder instead England full of Normans
Glad I didn't change my name to that!
Black Death and other deaths in wide range of colours
(Possible topic for thesis) What if Columbus had left
America alone (another possible topic for thesis)
The invention of gravity The invention of steam
       (Put kettle on, Ma)
American and French and Russian revolutions
railways end of slavery Votes for Women
radio and TV several World Wars Graduated with First
Class Honours Stayed for Postgraduate nailed Master's
degree (took ten minutes tops) Dean begged me to teach
while reading for Doctorate but had other haddock to fry
Ain't it just like me to travel the unpredictable path?
Took part-time job
in faux British fish & chip & kebab shop
catering to tourist trade Culinary skills had lain
too long dormant Increased turnover
of establishment by some 64%
according to endlessly grateful proprietor Luigi
Very tired Slept like a pea in a pot
               Crack of dawn Swam in
ocean Frolicked on sand Sent postcard to Ma
Feeling arty again (I have often wondered if people
understand me) Signed up for crash course to study basics
of music ('Special Offer!!!') Thought I might write
a few tunes Loads of theory re rhythm melody harmony
timbre dynamics texture form plus some vocabulary
probably useful when bumping into other musicians
Would be speaking same language
Grave slow and solemn Lento slowly Largo broadly
Adagio slow and stately (literally "at ease")
Adagietto rather slow Andante at a walking pace etcetera
Started to fall asleep during all this almost had second
thoughts On to strophic through-composed binary ternary
rondo Nodded right off at this point Woke up to sonata
theme and variations Lost and bored Not impressed by

teacher Figured I could do better on my own
Some teachers are in the wrong job Asked for refund
Didn't get it Argued a bit Still didn't get it Never mind
Taught myself piano violin cello guitar ukelele flute
piccolo trumpet bassoon oboe recorder harmonica kettle
drum triangle Established first one-man orchestra
Composed "First Symphony" "Second Piano
Sonata" and "Third Violin Concerto"
Decided to become singer/songwriter Wrote some
songs "All Of Your Legs" "My Babe Done Good"
"Rockin' By The Ocean" "Often I Have Wondered" "Kiss Me
Where It Hurts" "Thirteen Ways Of Looking At A Girl"
"Born In The Usual Way" "My Babe She Lied"
"The Lonely Minstrel" "Clasp Me To Your Bosom"
Need a few more for debut album Had sudden
flash of inspiration Cracking idea for opera
Love story with environmental theme Star-crossed lovers
one black one white one kind of neither one or the other
but had to put musical career on hold It was bedtime
Fell into bed humming Slept like an ear deaf to the world
                        Crack of dawn Swam in
ocean Frolicked on sand Sent postcard to Ma
Considered having crack at other art forms Cinema
sculpture theatre but who has the time? Also had
had enough of brain-straining foolery Bodily atrophy
is setting in It's as if dance class never happened
and perhaps it didn't Could be making all this up
Ran outside on to the playing fields for soccer
rugby (union and league) American football
baseball netball tennis crown green bowls bouncing
on bouncy castle polo golf 18-hole and crazy
Indoors for basketball squash badminton
Felt a bout of equestrianism coming on
working its way into my bones like I don't know
what simile to use here but I like horses (in theory)
Visited stables to meet some thoroughbreds Took part in
gymkhana (clear round, four faults, clear round)

Felt like racing steeplechase or flat not fussy
Always thought I was too tall to be a jockey
(I have often wondered how people take the measure of me)
Crouched a bit and got away with it Flew over the jumps
as if on blessèd wings What's that horse with wings? Oh
yes Pegasus Felt like I was on Pegasus Weather turned
very wintry a cold snap Great for luge bobsled ice hockey
skating speed and figure curling skiing alpine
jump and cross-country snowboarding Evening
took to the tables for chess draughts backgammon
poker bridge snap beat your neighbour out of doors
Monopoly Connect 4 Thanks to exercise of competitive
spirit slept like a badger in a badger box
                              Crack of dawn Swam in
ocean Frolicked on sand Sent postcard to Ma
Set about exploration of the kingdom republic or state
Was not sure Visited the suburbs business district
industrial area Roamed hinterland waste land
Who was the third walking always beside me?
Crossed moorland meadowland farmland winter
wonderland pasture wilderness forests woods
copses thickets Navigated rivers rapids
canals streams brooks waterfalls cataracts (sound of
which haunt me like a passion) lakes wetlands
mountains foothills plateaus (dissected and volcanic)
mesas valleys plains deserts ocean basin Had with me
field easel pochade box mini palette cups
brush washer brush holder tripod palette knife
Never leave home without them Ma always said
So stopped here and there to do some painting
en plein air Oils watercolours pastels acrylics ink wash
gouache Knocked off half a dozen decent pictures
An Edward Hopper roadside café
19th century hay cart Constable would have been proud of
A lovely horse in the style of George Stubbs
Landscape with a farmhouse in manner of Camille Pissarro
A field of poppies reminiscent of Claude Monet

Also a self-portrait (I have often wondered
how I see myself) Then a tribute or homage
to Pablo Pollock thrown in for good measure
I'll probably do some more
when I get home Slept like a still life
                    Crack of dawn Swam in
ocean Frolicked on sand Sent postcard to Ma
You would have enjoyed what's coming next
The finest garden and orchard ever seen
In it a place as fair as a maiden's chamber for canaries
parrots macaws budgerigars birds of paradise
with fine branches of trees for them to sit in
Two dovecotes palaces for turtle doves
Peacocks strolled endless perfect lawns
Six or seven fish ponds all railed about and full
Koi carp goldfish shubunkin sturgeon sunfish
Seven or eight fine fountains or water springs
Fruit of all sorts Oranges figs grapes apples pears plums
cherries bananas Palm trees weighed down with coconuts
Also filberts walnuts small nuts don't know their names
Took lodgings for the night (I have often wondered
if people can see me in the dark) Lodging house door
so low had to creep in on hands and knees
No chairs stool or bench to sit upon Food was brought
from out of the town by girls on bicycles
Comfortable words on their lips and fair promises
Danger of falling in love again Enjoyed eggs bread cheese
Also great store of fruit (cf. list above) Water was drawn
out of the well No beds so had to lay on a mat
on the ground Slept like a cuckoo in a clock
Woke up on the hour every hour
                    Crack of dawn Swam in
ocean Frolicked on sand Sent postcard to Ma
Have run out of postcards so am unable to write
which is a shame pity cause for regret disappointment
sorrow ruefulness perhaps even woe I don't know
It's the last day of the jollidays

Seems like good timing now great troubles
have chanced in these parts These troubles
trouble the people Of those which were of
the old queen's council or bore any love for her
some are in prison some are pinched in the purse
Others are sent for unto the people's new leader
an ill-omened creature with monkey face and monkish cowl
What shall become of them nobody knows
Rain ricochets off the ground into sky begetting rainbow
upon rainbow Elephants the colour of frogs or fog
the colour of elephants clambering out of the salt mines
Things are turning interesting slightly bewildering
Invited to séance by a tiny but well-formed nymphet
who scampered off teasingly into the trees
White shadows forming in half-light Surrounded by
children of the most grotesque disabilities
It near sickens me to think anyone could laugh at them
but it happens The mental health of some of these people
reminds me of home (I have often wondered where
I belong) What else is there to say? The natives believe
great troubles are sent by the gods but think
they will in time overcome them which I guess is
good It's good to be optimistic (I have often wondered
why people consider me curmudgeonly) Probably
wise to be leaving Pack trunk Double check nothing
left or right in room by mistake error brain failure
amnesia There's no coming back Settle hotel bill No
did not use mini-bar On way out notice advertisement
for cookery classes ('Special Offer!!!') but
cf. "Culinary skills had lain too long dormant"
so not in the least disappointed Take
horse-drawn taxi to railway station airport
harbour God give me good hour
and may I be well to speed with a merry heart
returning home to Ma

Martin Stannard lives
in quiet retirement
in Nottingham
with his cat, Xiao Mei.

www.martinstannard.com